ESSENTIAL ELEMENTS
FOR BAND

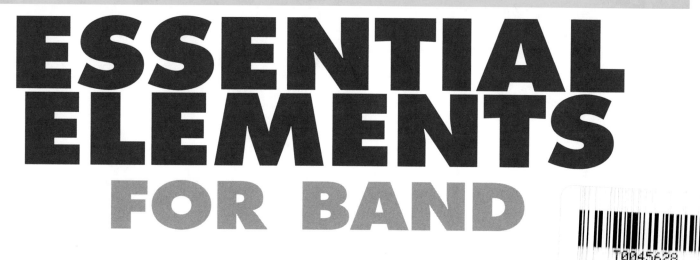

COMPREHENSIVE BAND METHOD

TIM LAUTZENHEISER

JOHN HIGGINS

CHARLES MENGHINI

PAUL LAVENDER

TOM C. RHODES

DON BIERSCHENK

To create an account, visit:
www.essentialelementsinteractive.com

STUDENT ACTIVATION CODE
E2CL-1474-2404-8718

ISBN 978-0-634-01288-4

HAL•LEONARD®
CORPORATION
7777 W. BLUEMOUND RD. P.O. BOX 13819 MILWAUKEE, WI 53213

REVIEW

	KEY SIGNATURE	TIME SIGNATURES	BREATH MARK		B	C	D	E	F	G	A

Key of C

NOTES	Whole	Half	Quarter	Eighths	REPEAT SIGN	TIE	SLUR	TEMPO MARKINGS
RESTS								Allegro Moderato

1. TECHNIQUE TRAX

2. SHOO FLY

American Folk Song

Allegro

3. THAILAND LULLABY

Thai Folk Song

Moderato

4. SHEPHERD'S HEY

English Folk Song

Moderato

5. THE CRAWDAD SONG

American Folk Song

Allegro

REVIEW

6. AMERICA/GOD SAVE THE QUEEN

Based on a Traditional Anthem

7. WEARING OF THE GREEN

Irish Folk Song

8. ROSES FROM THE SOUTH

Johann Strauss, Jr.

9. CRUISIN' THROUGH THE PARK

10. TRUMPET VOLUNTARY — Duet

Jeremiah Clarke

4

REVIEW

MULTIPLE MEASURE REST	ACCENT	FERMATA	D.C. al FINE
2	>	𝄐	

Eighth Note & Eighth Rest	Eighth Rest & Eighth Note	Eighth Note & Dotted Quarter Note

ENHARMONICS

11. CHROMA-ZONE

Fine

D.C. al Fine

12. BILLY BOY

American Folk Song

Moderato

13. TECHNIQUE TRAX

Allegro

14. SALSA SIESTA – Duet

Moderato

Staccato

♩ Staccato notes are played lightly and with separation. They are marked with a dot above or below the note.

15. TREADING LIGHTLY

Moderato

Tenuto

♩ Tenuto notes are played smoothly and connected, holding each note until the next is played. They are marked with a straight line above or below the note.

16. SMOOTH MOVE

Moderato

17. SHIFTING GEARS – New Note

Practice long tones on all new notes.

A

Moderato

18. TALLIS CANON (Round)

Moderato

Thomas Tallis

Sightreading

Sightreading means playing a musical piece for the first time. The key to sightreading success is to know what to look for *before* you play. Use the word **S-T-A-R-S** to remind yourself what to look for, and eventually your band will become sightreading STARS!

S — **Sharps or flats** in the key signature
T — **Time signature** and **tempo markings**
A — **Accidentals** not found in the key signature
R — **Rhythms**, silently counting the more difficult notes and rests
S — **Signs**, including dynamics, articulations, repeats and endings

19. SIGHTREADING CHALLENGE

Moderato

DAILY WARM-UPS

WORK-OUTS FOR TONE & TECHNIQUE

20. TONE BUILDER

21. FLEXIBILITY STUDY

22. TECHNIQUE TRAX

23. CHORALE

Johann Sebastian Bach

Andante

24. GRANDFATHER'S CLOCK

Henry C. Work

Allegro

Ritardando

ritard. (or) *rit.* - Gradually slower

25. GLOW WORM

Paul Lincke

Allegretto ◁ *Usually a little slower than Allegro, and with a lighter style.*

rit. ◁ *Watch your director.*

26. ALMA MATER
A.C. Weekes, W.M. Smith, H.S. Thompson

The Scottish folk song *Loch Lomond* is credited to an anonymous soldier who was imprisoned and awaiting execution. In it he writes of his desire to return home to his family and the breathtaking beauty of Loch (Lake) Lomond, a lake in Scotland. Located in the southern highlands, the lake is almost entirely surrounded by hills. One of these is Ben Lomond, a peak 3,192 feet high.

HISTORY

27. LOCH LOMOND
Scottish Folk Song

Key Changes

If a key signature changes during a piece of music, you will usually see a thin double bar line at the **key change**. You may also see natural signs reminding you to "cancel" previous sharps or flats. Keep playing, using the correct notes indicated in the *new* key signature.

THEORY

28. MOLLY MALONE
Irish Folk Song

Dynamics

cresc. = crescendo (or)
decresc. = decrescendo (or)

29. RISE AND FALL

30. NO COMPARISON

31. SIGHTREADING CHALLENGE
Remember the S-T-A-R-S guidelines.

THEORY

¢ Time Signature
Cut Time (Alla Breve)

$\begin{array}{c} & & \end{array}$ ¢ or $\frac{2}{2}$ = **2 beats** per measure
= **Half** note gets one beat

𝅝 = 2 beats
𝅗𝅥 = 1 beat
♩ = ½ beat

32. RHYTHM RAP *Clap the rhythm while counting and tapping.*

Clap

1 & 2 & 1 & 2 & 1 & 2 & 1 & 2 & 1 & 2 & 1 & 2 & 1 & 2 & 1 & 2 & 1 & 2 &

33. A CUT ABOVE

1 & 2 & 1 & 2 & 1 & 2 & 1 & 2 & 1 & 2 & 1 & 2 & 1 & 2 & 1 & 2 & 1 & 2 &

34. TWO-FOUR YANKEE DOODLE

American Folk Song

Moderato

mf

35. CUT TIME YANKEE DOODLE

American Folk Song

Moderato

mf

36. MARIANNE

Jamaican Folk Song

Moderato

1. 2.

p cresc.   *f decresc.*   *p*

37. THE VICTORS

Louis Elbel

March Tempo

f

Count ➤ **1 & 2 &**

1. 2.

1 & 2 &

38. ESSENTIAL CREATIVITY *Write this example in cut time ¢ before playing.*

Allegro

f

Allegro

Dynamics

mp — *mezzo piano* (moderately soft)

Use full breath support at all dynamic levels.

p — *mp* — *mf* — *f*

39. A - ROVING

Syncopation

Syncopation occurs when an accent or emphasis is given to a note that is not on a strong beat. This type of "off-beat" feel is common in many popular and classical styles.

40. RHYTHM RAP

41. IN SYNC

42. LA ROCA

Puerto Rican Folk Song

American composer **George M. Cohan** (1878–1942) was also a popular author, producer, director and performer. He helped develop a popular form of American musical theater now known as musical comedy. He is also considered to be one of the most famous composers of American patriotic songs, earning the Congressional Medal of Honor in 1917 for his song *Over There*. Many of his songs became morale boosters when the United States entered World War I in that same year.

43. ESSENTIAL ELEMENTS QUIZ – YOU'RE A GRAND OLD FLAG

Words and Music by George M. Cohan

THEORY

New Key Signature

This key signature indicates your **Key of D** (Concert C).
Play all F's as F-sharp and all C's as C-sharp.

44. KEY MOMENT – New Note

Right Hand fingering

D Scale   ▽ C♯   *Arpeggio*

45. THE MINSTREL BOY

Irish Folk Song

Andante

mp

46. CLOSE CALL – New Note

▽ C♯

47. VICTORY MARCH

M. J. Shea

March Tempo

f   △ Chromatic (Chr.) F♯

THEORY

Cut Time Syncopation

Compare the notation of the melody below with *Victory March* above. Should they sound the same?

48. WINNING STREAK

M. J. Shea

March Tempo

f   △ Chr.

49. SIGHTREADING CHALLENGE

Remember the S-T-A-R-S guidelines.

Moderato

mp   *mf*

Sixteenth Notes

4 sixteenth notes = 1 Beat
Each sixteenth note = ¼ Beat

1 e & a

1 e & a 2 e & a

A single sixteenth note has 2 flags on the stem.

50. RHYTHM RAP

Clap

1 & 2 & 3 e & a 4 & | 1 & 2 & 3 e & a 4 & | 1 & 2 e & a 3 & 4 & | 1 & 2 e & a 3 & 4 &

51. SIXTEENTH NOTE FANFARE

1 & 2 & 3 e & a 4 & | 1 & 2 & 3 e & a 4 & | 1 & 2 e & a 3 & 4 & | 1 & 2 e & a 3 & 4 &

52. MOVING ALONG

53. BACK AND FORTH – Duet

54. COMIN' ROUND THE MOUNTAIN VARIATIONS

American Folk Song

Moderato

f

55. ESSENTIAL ELEMENTS QUIZ

Moderato

f

PERFORMANCE SPOTLIGHT

56. WARM-UP CHORALE

J. S. Bach/Arr. by John Higgins

57. THE THUNDERER – Band Arrangement

John Philip Sousa
Arr. by John Higgins

Reproduced by Permission of Boosey & Hawkes Music Publishers Ltd.

58. HILL AND GULLY RIDER – Band Arrangement

Jamaican Folk Song
Arr. by John Higgins

59. SHENANDOAH – Band Arrangement

American Folk Song
Arr. by John Higgins

PERFORMANCE SPOTLIGHT

60. LAS MAÑANITAS – Band Arrangement

Mexican Folk Song
Arr. by John Higgins

61. RONDEAU – Band Arrangement

Jean-Joseph Mouret
Arr. by John Higgins

D.S. al Fine–Go back to the sign (𝄋) and play until **Fine**.

62. ROCK.COM – Encore Band Arrangement

John Higgins

69. RHYTHM RAP

70. RHYTHM ETUDE

71. BATTLE STATIONS

72. ENGLISH DANCE

73. BIG ROCK CANDY MOUNTAIN

American Folk Song

74. ESSENTIAL ELEMENTS QUIZ

Rallentando   *rall.* – Gradually slower (same as ritardando)

75. SIMPLE SONG – Duet

Watch your director

76. LINE DANCE

77. TECHNIQUE TRAX

Keep 16ths steady

78. THE GALWAY PIPER

Irish Reel

79. MANHATTAN BEACH MARCH

John Philip Sousa

80. SIGHTREADING CHALLENGE   *Remember the S-T-A-R-S guidelines.*

81. RHYTHM RAP

82. MARCHING ALONG

83. FANFARE FOR BAND – Trio

84. O TANNENBAUM

German Carol

85. S'VIVON

Traditional Hanukkah Song

86. GOOD KING WENCESLAS

English Carol

DAILY WARM-UPS

WORK-OUTS FOR TONE & TECHNIQUE

87. TONE BUILDER *Play at a very slow tempo.*

88. FLEXIBILITY STUDY *Try "Right Hand B" for smoother technique.*

89. TECHNIQUE TRAX

90. CHORALE

Johann Sebastian Bach

HISTORY

French composer **Georges Bizet** (1838–1875) entered the Paris Conservatory to study music when he was only ten years old. There he won many awards for voice, piano, organ, and composition. Bizet's best known composition is the opera *Carmen,* which was first performed in 1875. *Carmen* tells the story of a band of Gypsies, soldiers, smugglers, and outlaws. Originally criticized for its realism on stage, it was soon hailed as the most popular French opera ever written.

91. TOREADOR SONG (from CARMEN)

Georges Bizet

92. LA CUMPARSITA – New Note (Enharmonic)

G. Rodriguez

Enharmonics

93. THE YELLOW ROSE OF TEXAS *Check the key signature.*

American Folk Song

94. SCALE STUDY

F Scale

▾ *Check rhythm*

Until 1974 Australia's official national anthem was *God Save The Queen*. A competition was held in 1973 to compose a new anthem, but none of the entries met with the judges' approval. Finally the government asked the public to vote, choosing from among Australia's 3 most popular patriotic songs. After easily defeating *Waltzing Matilda* and *God Save The Queen*, *Advance Australia Fair* was officially declared the national anthem of Australia on April 19, 1974.

HISTORY

95. ADVANCE AUSTRALIA FAIR

Peter Dodds McCormick

rit.   *a tempo*
△ *Resume previous tempo*

96. ESSENTIAL CREATIVITY

Arrange the melody of "America (My Country 'Tis Of Thee)" for your instrument. Write out the first line (6 measures).
Your first note is G. ADD: Key signature—key of G • Time signature—3/4 • Tempo and dynamic markings.

Play the completed line on your instrument to hear your own version.

97. AMERICAN PATROL

F. W. Meacham

Moderato

98. ARIA (from MARRIAGE OF FIGARO)

Wolfgang Amadeus Mozart

Moderato

HISTORY

American composer **John Philip Sousa** (1854–1932) was best known for his brilliant band marches. Sousa wrote 136 marches, including *The Stars and Stripes Forever,* which was declared the official march of the United States of America in 1987.

99. THE STARS AND STRIPES FOREVER – New Note

John Philip Sousa

F♯

Right Hand

March Tempo

Check rhythm

17   ▲ F♯

100. SIGHTREADING CHALLENGE *Remember the S-T-A-R-S guidelines.*

Moderato

⁶⁄₈ Time Signature

 = **6 beats** per measure
= **Eighth** note gets one beat

♪ = 1 beat   ♩ = 2 beats
♩. = 3 beats   ♩. = 6 beats

6/8 time is usually played with a slight emphasis on the **1st** and **4th** beats of each measure. This divides the measure into 2 groups of 3 beats each. In faster music, these two primary beats will make the music feel like it's counted "in 2."

101. RHYTHM RAP *Clap the rhythm while counting and tapping.*

102. LAZY DAY

103. ROW YOUR BOAT

104. JOLLY GOOD FELLOW

105. CHANSON

French Folk Song

106. ESSENTIAL ELEMENTS QUIZ – WHEN JOHNNY COMES MARCHING HOME

American Folk Song

THEORY

More Enharmonics

Remember that notes which sound the same but have different letter names are called **enharmonics**. These are some common enharmonics that you'll use in the exercises below.

More Chromatics

The smallest distance between two notes is a half-step, and a scale made up of consecutive half-steps is a **chromatic scale.** These are usually written with **enharmonic** notes—sharps when going up and flats when going down.

Learn to use the suggested **chromatic fingerings** for smoother technique in chromatic note combinations.

107. CHROMATIC SCALE

Practice slowly until you are sure of all the fingerings.

F♯/G♭

Chromatic fingering

△ Chr.

108. TECHNIQUE TRAX

Chr.   Chr.

Chr.   Chr.

HISTORY

A **Habañera** is a Cuban dance and song form in slow 2/4 meter. It is named after the city of Havana, the capital of Cuba. Made popular in the New World in the early 19th Century, it was later carried over to Spain. There the rhythms of the Habañera were incorporated into many styles of Latin music. One of the most famous Habañeras is heard in Bizet's *Carmen,* written in 1875.

109. HABAÑERA (from CARMEN)

C♯/D♭

Georges Bizet

Left Hand fingering

Andante

mf △ Left Hand   *decresc.*

p   mf △ Left   *decresc.   p*

110. CHROMATIC CRESCENDO

Moderato

p   cresc.   Chr.   Chr.

L   Chr.

mf   *f*   *rall.*

111. TURKISH MARCH (from THE RUINS OF ATHENS)

Ludwig van Beethoven

112. THE OVERLANDER

Australian Folk Song

113. STACCATO STUDY

114. YANKEE DOODLE DANDY

Words and Music by George M. Cohan

115. SIGHTREADING CHALLENGE

Remember the **S-T-A-R-S** guidelines:
S – Sharps or flats in the key signature, **T** – Time signature and tempos, **A** – Accidentals, **R** – Rhythm, **S** – Signs

Triplets

A **triplet** is a group of **3** notes played in the space of **2**. In $\frac{2}{4}$, $\frac{3}{4}$, or $\frac{4}{4}$ time, an eighth note triplet is spread evenly across one beat.

116. RHYTHM RAP

117. THREE TO GET READY

118. TRIPLET STUDY

119. MARCH (from THE NUTCRACKER) – Duet

Peter I. Tchaikovsky

120. ESSENTIAL ELEMENTS QUIZ – THEME FROM FAUST

Charles Gounod

121. SCALE STUDY

122. OVER THE RIVER AND THROUGH THE WOODS

American Folk Song

123. RHYTHM RAP

124. ON THE MOVE

125. HIGHER GROUND

126. ESSENTIAL ELEMENTS QUIZ

The first known printing of the lyrics and music to **The Marines' Hymn** dates from August 1, 1918. An unknown author is believed to have taken the opening words of the song from the words on the Marine Corps flag, "From the halls of Montezuma to the shores of Tripoli." The music was taken from "Genevieve de Brabant," by the operetta composer Jacques Offenbach.

127. THE MARINES' HYMN

D.S. al Fine

Play until you see the **D.S. al Fine**. Then go back to the sign (𝄋) and play until the word **Fine**. **D.S.** is the abbreviation for **Dal Segno**, or "from the sign," and **Fine** means "the end."

128. D.S. MARCH

Accelerando

accel. – Gradually faster.

129. CAN–CAN

Jacques Offenbach

accel.

△ *Watch your director.*

130. TARANTELLA

Allegro

Italian Folk Song

f ▷ Pick-up   *mf*

> The **waltz** is a dance in moderate 3/4 time which developed around 1800 from the Ländler, an Austrian peasant dance. Austrian composer **Johann Strauss, Jr.** (1825–1899) composed over 400 waltzes. These include such famous pieces as *The Blue Danube, Tales From the Vienna Woods* and *Emperor Waltz.*

HISTORY

131. EMPEROR WALTZ

Andantino ◁ *Tempo between Andante and Moderato.*

Johann Strauss, Jr.

Legato Style

legato – Played in a smooth, connected style.

132. ENGLISH DANCE – Duet

Johann Christian Bach

133. ESSENTIAL ELEMENTS QUIZ – BRITISH GRENADIERS

Allegretto

Traditional

134. NASSAU BOUND

Bahamian Folk Song

Count ▶ 1 & 2 & 3 & 4 &

135. UNFINISHED SYMPHONY THEME

Franz Schubert

136. RHYTHM STUDY

Measure Repeat   ⁒   Repeat the previous measure once for each **Measure Repeat** sign.

---

137. COUNTRY GARDENS

English Folk Song

138. JOSHUA

African-American Spiritual

139. LISTEN TO THE MOCKINGBIRD

Alice Hawthorne

140. ANCHORS AWEIGH

Capt. A.H. Miles and C.A. Zimmerman

141. GREENSLEEVES

English Folk Song

142. THE LONG CLIMB – New Notes

△ Measure Repeat

143. THE BLUE BELLS OF SCOTLAND

Scottish Folk Song

Major and Minor

The scales you've already learned are called **Major** scales. They all follow the same pattern, with **half-steps** between notes 3–4 and between notes 7–8.

Natural Minor scales follow a different pattern, with **half-steps** between notes 2–3 and 5–6. The **A Minor** scale uses the same key signature as **C Major**.

Another type of minor scale is called **Harmonic Minor**, which adds an accidental to raise the **7th** note by a half-step. Compare the scales on the right.

See page 37 for additional minor scales.

THEORY

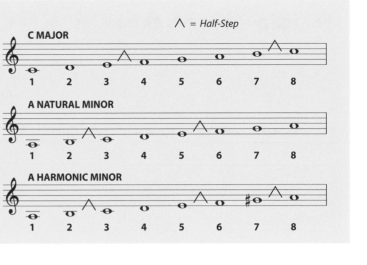

---

144. NATURAL MINOR SCALE

---

145. FINALE FROM "NEW WORLD SYMPHONY"

Antonin Dvořák

---

146. HARMONIC MINOR SCALE – New Note

G♯/A♭

---

147. HUNGARIAN DANCE NO. 5

Johannes Brahms

---

148. POMP AND CIRCUMSTANCE (LAND OF HOPE AND GLORY)

Edward Elgar

PERFORMANCE SPOTLIGHT

D.S. al Coda Play until you see the **D.S. al Coda**. Then go back to the sign (𝄋) and play until the **Coda Sign** ("To Coda" ⊕). Skip directly to the **Coda** and play until the end.

149. SIMPLE GIFTS – Band Arrangement

Shaker Folk Song
Arr. by John Higgins

150. SEMPER FIDELIS – Band Arrangement

John Philip Sousa
Arr. by John Higgins

PERFORMANCE SPOTLIGHT

151. DANNY BOY – Band Arrangement

Irish Folk Song
Arr. by John Higgins

152. TAKE ME OUT TO THE BALL GAME – Band Arrangement

By Jack Norworth and Harry von Tilzer
Arr. by John Higgins

PERFORMANCE SPOTLIGHT

153. SERENGETI (AFRICAN RHAPSODY) – Band Arrangement

John Higgins

RUBANK® STUDIES

154. CHORALE (Concert B♭)

155. CHORALE (Concert E♭)

156. CHORALE (Concert F)

157. CHORALE (Concert A♭)

158. CHORALE (Concert C)

CLARINET KEY OF C (CONCERT B♭)

159.

160.

161.

162.

RUBANK® STUDIES

CLARINET KEY OF F (CONCERT E♭)

163.

164.

165.

166.

CLARINET KEY OF G (CONCERT F)

167.

168.

169.

170.

Chr.   *Chr.*

RUBANK® STUDIES

CLARINET KEY OF B♭ (CONCERT A♭)

171.

172.

173.

174.

CLARINET KEY OF D (CONCERT C)

175.

176.

177.

178.

Chr.   Chr.

RUBANK® STUDIES

CLARINET KEY OF A MINOR (CONCERT G MINOR)

179.

180.

CLARINET KEY OF D MINOR (CONCERT C MINOR)

181.

182.

CLARINET KEY OF E MINOR (CONCERT D MINOR)

183.

184.

CHROMATIC SCALES

185.

186.

INDIVIDUAL STUDY – Clarinet

INDIVIDUAL STUDY – Clarinet

194. LEFT HAND STUDY

CD Track 63

Right Hand Down - - - - - - - - - - - - - -

Right Hand Down - - - - - - - - - - - - - -

R   R

Try "Right Hand B" for smoother technique.

195. BACK AND FORTH

CD Track 64

196. CROSSOVER

CD Track 65

R R R   R

197. ARTICULATION STUDY

CD Track 66

198. ARPEGGIO CHALLENGE NO. 1

CD Track 67

R   R   R

R   R

199. ARPEGGIO CHALLENGE NO. 2

CD Track 68

R   R

R R

INDIVIDUAL STUDY – Clarinet

Solo with Piano Accompaniment

You can perform this solo with the piano accompaniment on the following page.

Grace Note ♪

A **Grace Note** is a musical *ornament*—a small, quick note attached to a larger note by a slur. It is usually played just before the beat, and its brief time value is not counted in the measure.

200. HUNTERS' CHORUS from "Der Freischütz" – Clarinet Solo *CD Track 69*

Carl Maria von Weber
Arr. by Henry W. Davis

INDIVIDUAL STUDY – Clarinet

200. HUNTERS' CHORUS from "Der Freischütz" – Piano Accompaniment
CD Track 70

Carl Maria von Weber
Arr. by Henry W. Davis

RHYTHM STUDIES

RHYTHM STUDIES

CREATING MUSIC

Theme and Variation

Theme and Variation is a technique used by composers and arrangers to create interesting musical ideas that are "varied" from an established melody, or "theme." Play the following theme and two variations to hear how the arranger has created new phrases based on the original melody.

1. THEME

"Simple Gifts"

VARIATION 1 *Adding some notes • Changing some rhythms*

VARIATION 2 *Removing notes • Changing rhythms • Adding accents • Adding notes*

2. THEME AND YOUR VARIATION

Write your own variation of this theme. Use your instrument to hear and try different ideas.

"Oh, Susanna"

Theme

Your Variation

Blues Improvisation

Improvisation using a **Blues Scale** is an important part of jazz and popular music. Musicians use combinations of these notes and various rhythms to create their own spontaneous solos over a 12 measure progression of chords.

Blues Scale

3. LET'S JAM *Use the indicated notes from the Blues Scale to create your own solo to play with the accompaniment (Line B).*

You can mark your progress through the book on this page. Fill in the stars as instructed by your band director.

ESSENTIAL ELEMENTS

STAR ACHIEVER

NAME_____

1. Page 2–4, Review
2. Page 5, Sightreading Challenge, No. 19
3. Page 6, Daily Warm-Ups
4. Page 7, Sightreading Challenge, No. 31
5. Page 8, Essential Creativity, No. 38
6. Page 9, EE Quiz, No. 43
7. Page 10, Sightreading Challenge, No. 49
8. Page 11, EE Quiz, No. 55
9. Page 12–13, Performance Spotlight
10. Page 15, EE Quiz, No. 74
11. Page 16, Sightreading Challenge, No. 80
12. Page 18, Daily Warm-Ups
13. Page 19, Essential Creativity, No. 96
14. Page 20, Sightreading Challenge, No. 100

15. Page 21, EE Quiz, No. 106
16. Page 22, Chromatic Scale, No. 107
17. Page 23, Sightreading Challenge, No. 115
18. Page 24, EE Quiz, No. 120
19. Page 25, EE Quiz, No. 126
20. Page 27, EE Quiz, No. 133
21. Page 30, Natural Minor Scale, No. 144
22. Page 30, Harmonic Minor Scale, No. 146
23. Page 30, Pomp and Circumstance, No. 148
24. Page 31, Performance Spotlight
25. Page 32, Performance Spotlight
26. Page 33, Performance Spotlight
27. Page 38–39, Individual Study
28. Page 40, Performance Spotlight

MUSIC — AN ESSENTIAL ELEMENT OF LIFE

FINGERING CHART

CLARINET

Instrument Care Reminders

Before putting your instrument back in its case after playing, do the following:

- Remove the reed, wipe off excess moisture and return it to the reed case.
- Remove the mouthpiece and wipe the inside with a clean cloth. Once a week, wash the mouthpiece with warm tap water. Dry thoroughly.
- Drop a weighted chamois or cotton swab into the bell and pull it out through the barrel.
- Carefully twist off the barrel and dry off any additional moisture. Place it in the case.
- Gently twist the upper and lower sections apart, with the bell still attached. Place the upper section in the case.
- Remove the bell and place the bell and lower section back into the case.
- As you put each piece back in the case, check to be sure they are dry.
- Your case is designed to hold only specific objects. If you try to force anything else into the case, it may damage your instrument.

○ = Open
● = Pressed down

Alternate fingerings are used in certain situations to allow for smoother technique. These are shown to the right of the more common fingerings.

Instrument courtesy of Yamaha Corporation of America, Band and Orchestral Division

FINGERING CHART

Bb CLARINET

REFERENCE INDEX